MEGA MODEL

T. REX

WRITTEN BY SCOTT FORBES

SCHOLASTIC
www.scholastic.com

THIS IS A CARLTON BOOK

© Carlton Books Limited 2015

This edition published by Scholastic Inc.,
557 Broadway, New York, NY 10012,
by arrangement with Carlton Books Limited.

Scholastic and associated logos are trademarks and/or
registered trademarks of Scholastic Inc.

Distributed by Scholastic Canada, Ltd., Markham, Ontario

10 9 8 7 6 5 4 3 2 1

ISBN: 978-0-545-85488-7

Printed in Heshan, China

Author: Scott Forbes
Senior Editor: Alexandra Koken
Creative Director: Clare Baggaley
Paper Engineer: Jonathan Lambert
Designers: Jonathan Lambert and Ceri Hurst
Production: Charlotte Cade

CONTENTS

YOUR **T. REX** MODEL PIECES

Before you start building your T. rex, make sure you lay out all the pieces as shown below. This will make the model easier to assemble.

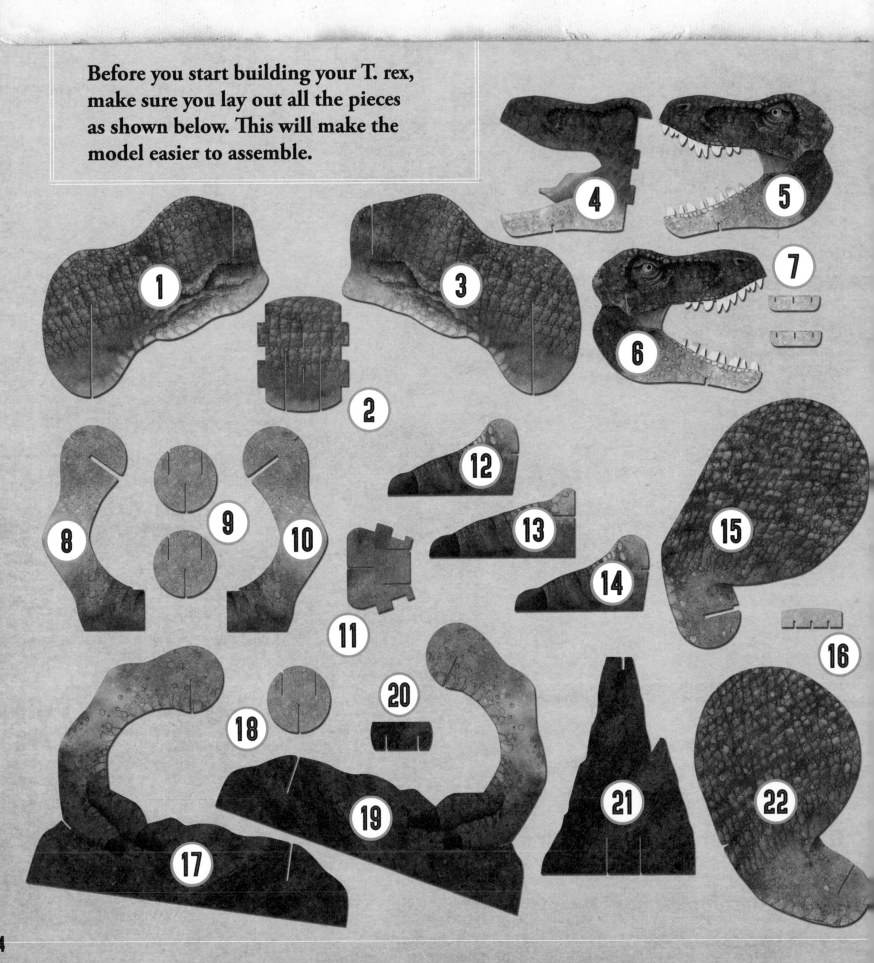

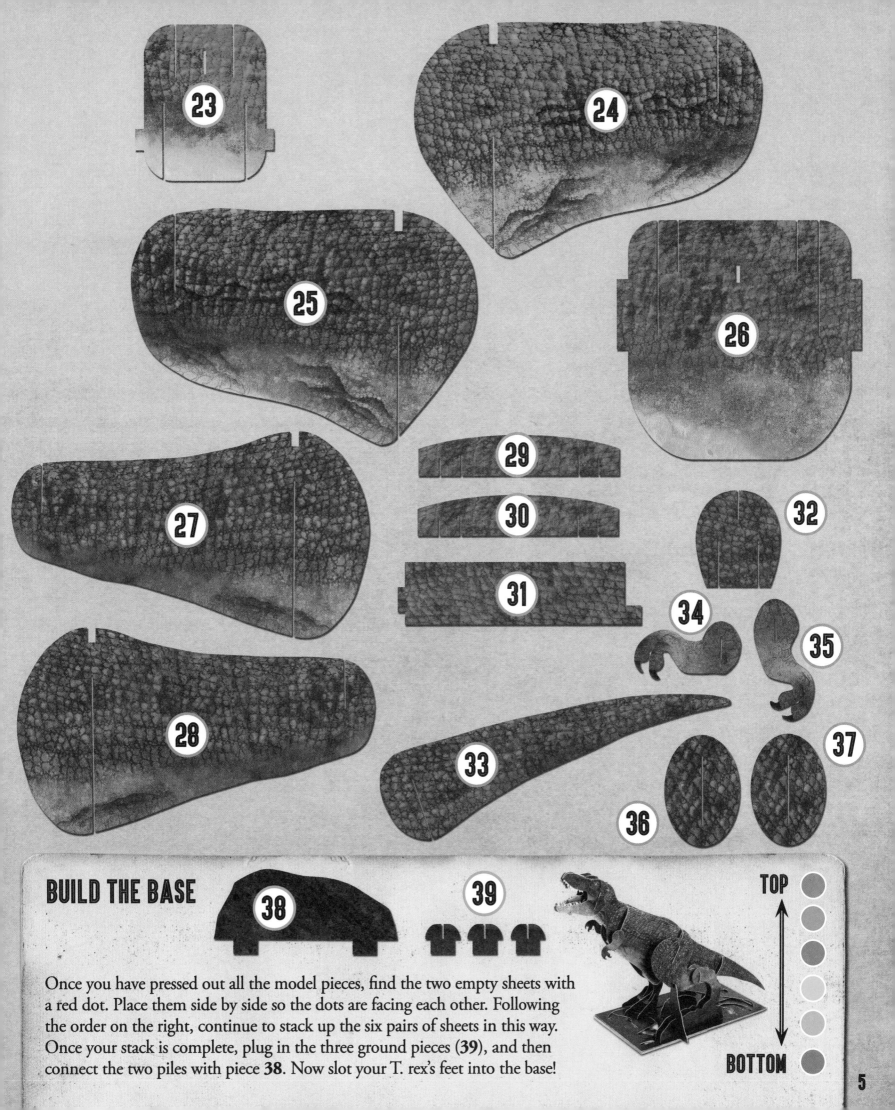

BUILD THE BASE

Once you have pressed out all the model pieces, find the two empty sheets with a red dot. Place them side by side so the dots are facing each other. Following the order on the right, continue to stack up the six pairs of sheets in this way. Once your stack is complete, plug in the three ground pieces (**39**), and then connect the two piles with piece **38**. Now slot your T. rex's feet into the base!

TOP

BOTTOM

5

HOW TO BUILD YOUR T. REX

HEAD ASSEMBLY

YOU WILL NEED:

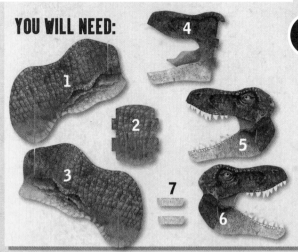

1 Push **2** onto the smaller slit on **1**.

2 Now push the short slit on **3** onto **2**, so that it faces the same way as **1**.

RIGHT LEG ASSEMBLY

YOU WILL NEED:

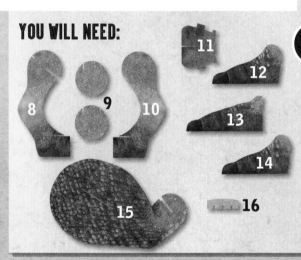

1 Hold both **9**s together with the single slits at the bottom. Push the curved ends of **8** and **10** onto the **9**s.

2 Slot **11** onto the opposite ends of **8** and **10**.

LEFT LEG ASSEMBLY

YOU WILL NEED:

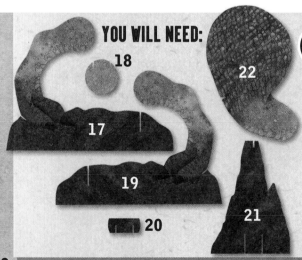

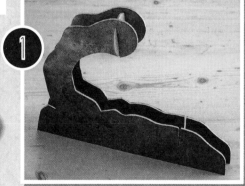

1 Push the narrow ends of **17** and **19** onto the two slits on the same side of **18**.

2 Add piece **20** to lock the foot in position. The connected pieces should stand up like this.

3 Push **4** into the middle of **2**, facing away from **1** and **3**. Push **5** onto the side of **2**, eye facing out.

4 Slot **6** onto the other side of **2** to complete the face.

5 Gently push both **7s** onto the underside of **4**, **5**, and **6** to support the jaw.

3 With the foot standing up as shown, slot **12** onto the tab on the closer side of **11**.

4 Slide **13** onto the slit in the middle of **11**, and **14** onto the tab on the far side of **11**.

5 Push the narrow end of **15** onto the final slit on **9**. Gently push **16** onto **8**, **10**, and **15** to strengthen the knee as shown.

3 Push the narrow end of **22** onto **18** from below.

4 Slide **21** onto the front of **17** and **19** to support the leg.

BODY ASSEMBLY

YOU WILL NEED:

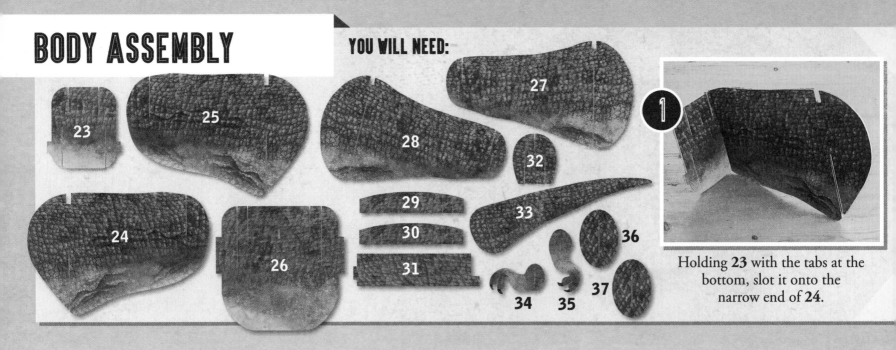

1

Holding **23** with the tabs at the bottom, slot it onto the narrow end of **24**.

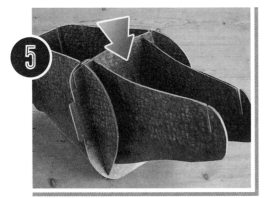

5

Slot **29** onto the notches on **24**, **25**, **27**, and **28**, as shown, to lock them together.

6

Turn the model around so that the tail is facing away from you.

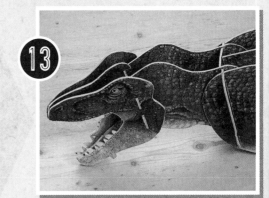

7

Use **30** to lock the pieces together as in **step 5**. Push hard to slot **30** on the opposite side of **26** to **29**.

11

Push **32** onto the ends of **27** and **28** to form the tail brace, as shown.

12

Slot **33** into the top slit on **32** to complete the tail.

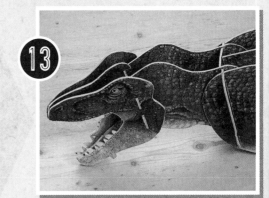

13

At the other end of the model, push pieces **1** and **3** (on the neck) onto the top of **23**.

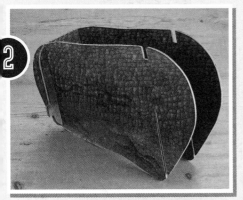

2

Push the other slit on the bottom of **23** onto the narrow end of **25**, as shown.

3

Slot the other ends of **24** and **25** into the long slits on **26**, as shown.

4

Push the wide ends of **27** and **28** onto **26** to start the tail.

8

Push the tab that sticks out from the bottom of **31** into the hole in **26**, inside the body area.

9

Slot the other end of **31** into the hole in **23**.

10

The body should look like this.

14

On the T. rex's shoulders, push **34** onto **23**, and repeat with **35** on the other side.

15

Add the legs onto the hip joints. Once done add pieces **36** and **37** over the tabs to secure the legs.

16

MARVEL AT YOUR MIGHTY T. REX!

DINO STAR!

Huge head with massive, powerful jaws and long teeth

WITHOUT A DOUBT, TYRANNOSAURUS REX—ALSO KNOWN AS T. REX—IS THE MOST FAMOUS DINOSAUR OF ALL TIME. It has appeared in countless movies, TV shows, and advertisements. Dozens of artists have painted it. Millions of people have admired its bones in museums. And its image pops up on everything from T-shirts to pajamas. Which is kind of strange, since T. rex is not exactly cuddly!

Long, thick tail held above the ground as it walked or ran

CATCHING OUR EYE

T. rex first caught the public's attention after a collector named Barnum Brown discovered large dinosaur bones in the western United States in 1902. He sent them to the American Museum of Natural History in New York City.

There, they were assembled as a skeleton and the dinosaur was named Tyrannosaurus rex, which means "tyrant lizard king" (a tyrant is a cruel ruler). When the skeleton was put on display, people were shocked and amazed by how big and frightening it was. They had never seen anything like it!

NAME: Tyrannosaurus rex
NICKNAME: T. rex

PLACE OF BIRTH: North America
DATE OF BIRTH: About 68 million years ago

HEIGHT: 13 ft. (4m)
LENGTH: 40 ft. (12m)
WEIGHT: 6½–9 tons

HOBBIES: Hunting and eating other dinosaurs

Strong legs with large claws on feet

BIG AT THE BOX OFFICE

Because of its amazing size and terrifying teeth, T. rex has appeared in many movies. It first appeared a century ago in an early special-effects movie called *The Ghost of Slumber Mountain* (1918), then battled a giant gorilla in *King Kong* (1933). More recently it terrified audiences around the world in *Jurassic Park* (1993) and its sequels, *The Lost World* (1997) and *Jurassic Park 3* (2011). A living T. rex skeleton caused havoc in the *Night at the Museum* movies (2006, 2014), too.

Tiny arms, with two long claws on each hand

REAL-LIFE T. REX

In real life, Tyrannosaurus rex was a ferocious killer—just about the last dinosaur you'd really want to meet! As tall and long as a double-decker bus, it lived almost 68 million years ago in what is now western North America, during a time known as the Cretaceous period.

BUILT TO KILL

BACK IN THE CRETACEOUS PERIOD, T. REX LIVED ALONGSIDE DOZENS OF OTHER KINDS OF DINOSAURS, MANY OF THEM ALSO ENORMOUS.

Among the meat-eaters or predators, however, T. rex was the undisputed king. It spent most of its time hunting and catching other creatures—before ripping them apart with its massive jaws.

JAWS OF DEATH

T. rex's jaws were not only big, but also incredibly powerful—at least three times as strong as those of a modern great white shark. Experiments have shown that they could have crushed a small car. More than 50 teeth lined the jaws, some of them up to 7 inches (17.8 cm) long—like big bananas—and up to 1 foot (30.5 cm) long if you include the root.

Teeth like long daggers made deep wounds

If any teeth were lost, they were replaced by new ones

Jaws were more than 3 feet (1 m) long

ON THE PROWL

In T. rex's world, forests of conifer trees, similar to today's pines and firs, separated wide plains carpeted with ferns and shrubs. Using its strong sense of smell, T. rex crept through the trees—then charged out of cover to attack. Among its larger targets was Triceratops. However, this big herbivore could fight back with its long, sharp horns, and it often survived an attack.

LETHAL BITE

T. rex usually killed with a crunching bite to the neck. Then it used its huge teeth to tear its victim's body apart. In a single big bite it could gobble up 507 lbs. (230 kg) of meat—the equivalent weight of a female lion!

KILLER COUSIN

While T. rex ruled in what is now North America, other parts of the world had their own fearsome predators. And some were even bigger and scarier! South America's Giganotosaurus, which lived about 100 million years ago, was 3 feet (1 m) longer than T. Rex. And around the same time in what is now Africa lived what may have been the biggest land predator of all time: Spinosaurus. Almost twice as long as a bus and twice as heavy as an elephant, it had massive, crocodile-like jaws as big as a bathtub and a dramatic row of skin-covered spines along its back.

TYRANNOSAURUS REX

FALL OF THE KING

ROUGHLY 66 MILLION YEARS AGO, ALONG WITH ALMOST ALL OTHER DINOSAURS, T. REX SUDDENLY DISAPPEARED FROM EARTH. WHAT HAPPENED?

Scientists believe a huge asteroid—a rock from space—crashed into our planet. More than three-quarters of all living things were wiped out as a result of this collision. However, among the survivors were a number of animals related to the dinosaurs, some of which are still around today.

CATASTROPHIC COLLISION

Asteroids travel through space all the time, but very rarely do they collide with planets. The asteroid that struck Earth 66 million years ago was about 7 miles (11.25 km) wide and traveled at around 62,137 mph (100,000 kph)! The impact left a huge crater in the Earth that measures about 112 miles (180 km) across. This crater now lies off the east coast of Mexico.

END OF A WORLD

When the asteroid struck, it had a catastrophic effect. Immediately there were huge explosions that sparked widespread fires. The colossal collision also triggered earthquakes, which in turn caused tsunamis—towering waves that flooded large areas of land. At the same time, there were massive volcanic eruptions in what is now India. Smoke and dust filled the air, blocking out the sun and making Earth much colder. Most plants quickly died out, and the animals that fed on them starved.

GREAT ESCAPE

Creatures that lived in the sea or underground escaped the worst of the disaster. Some animals survived by moving to a safer area—birds could do this, of course, by flying. Others changed their behavior to cope with the new conditions. Mammals were particularly good at this. Soon they started to dominate the animal kingdom as they do today (you, of course, are a mammal!).

Flying reptiles survived the mass extinction

DINOSAURS TODAY

There are some animals alive today that look like dinosaurs, such as iguanas and crocodiles. But in fact these are only very distant cousins. The creatures that are most directly descended from dinosaurs are birds. So those cute little things fluttering around in your backyard are actually T. rex's closest living relatives.

It's hard to believe this is a dinosaur!

HOW TO FIND A T. REX

EVEN AFTER TENS OF MILLIONS OF YEARS, TRACES OF T. REX CAN STILL BE FOUND ON OUR PLANET. They include bones, claws, and teeth, as well as marks left on rocks and on other creatures' bones. Scientists called paleontologists look for these remains, known as fossils, in rock layers, then dig them out of the ground. Look in the right places, and you could find some, too!

WHERE TO LOOK

To find T. rex fossils, you need to look where T. rex used to live, and that was in North America. Most T. rex fossils have been discovered in the Rocky Mountains in the western United States. It was here, in South Dakota in 1990, that an amateur fossil hunter named Sue Hendrickson dug up the biggest and most complete T. rex skeleton ever found. Named "Sue" in her honor, the skeleton was later sold for more than $8 million US. But experts still aren't sure whether Sue (the dinosaur) was male or female!

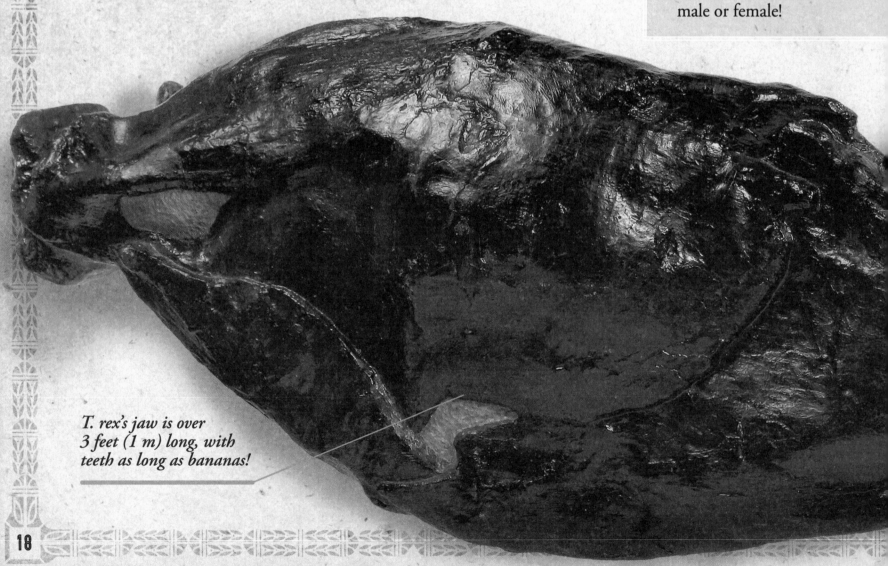

T. rex's jaw is over 3 feet (1 m) long, with teeth as long as bananas!

HOW TO DIG IT UP

To find fossils, look for sedimentary rocks, which are often made up of horizontal layers. Fossils are often found well-preserved within these layers. Paleontologists identify the dinosaur fossils they dig up by comparing them to others already discovered. Usually they can quickly tell if the find is of an existing species or a new one.

WHAT TO LOOK FOR

You won't find a whole T. rex anywhere, because all the soft parts of these creatures rotted away soon after they died. But their harder parts, like bones and teeth, often remained buried in the ground, where they sometimes became fossils. Other Tyrannosaurs disappeared but left their marks in rock layers. Among the more unusual kinds of fossils are dinosaur footprints and coprolites: fossilized dinosaur dung!

A STAR REBORN

Interesting fossils are put on display in museums. If a museum has many large bones from one kind of dinosaur, it may decide to build a complete skeleton, using plaster casts to fill in the gaps. You can see spectacular T. rex skeletons in many museums around the world. The museum with the biggest T. rex collection is the state of Montana's Museum of the Rockies. Only about 30 T. rex specimens have ever been found.

COLOSSAL FOSSIL

ARE YOU A T. REXPERT?

T. rex has thousands of young fans around the world and many of them already know a lot about this ferocious prehistoric predator. Are you one of them? Take this simple test to find out.

1 During which prehistoric period did T. rex live?
A Jurassic
B Triassic
C Cretaceous
D Victorian

2 What does T. rex's name mean?
A Tired old man
B Tall lizard called Rex
C Tyrant lizard king
D I'm coming to eat you

3 Which of these dinosaurs was around at the same time as T. rex?
A Triceratops
B Diplodocus
C Stegosaurus
D Seagull

4 How many legs did T. rex have?
A 1
B 2
C 4
D 13

5 T. rex was as big as …?
A You
B A man
C A horse
D A double-decker bus

6 How many claw-tipped fingers did T. rex have on each hand?
A Two
B Five
C Ten
D None—just two thumbs

7 What did T. rex do with its tail as it ran?
A Held onto it with one hand
B Dragged it along the ground
C Held it above the ground
D Scratched its back

8 Which of these dinosaurs was bigger than T. rex?
A Velociraptor
B Spinosaurus
C Pigeon
D Triceratops

9 T. rex's teeth were as big as…
A Yours
B Your fingers
C Carrots
D Bananas

10 What was T. rex's favorite food?
A Bananas
B Eggs
C Meat, meat, and more meat
D Fish

11 Which South American predator was similar to T. rex?

A   Argentinosaurus

B   Giganotosaurus

C   Spinosaurus

D   Gauchosaurus

12 Who found the first partial skeletons of T. rex?

A   Bill Brown

B   Barnum Brown

C   Barnum Barnum

D   Sue Hendrickson

13 How many specimens of T. rex have been found?

A   1

B   353

C   About 30

D   More than 800

14 Which is the best place to look for T. rex fossils?

A   Mexico

B   France

C   United States

D   Antarctica

15 What is a coprolite?

A   A very small Spanish dinosaur

B   A flashlight used by paleontologists to hunt for bones

C   A glue stick used for putting dinosaur skeletons together

D   Fossilized dinosaur dung

16 How much did the T. rex skeleton known as Sue cost when sold?

A $8 million US

B $8,000 US

C $800,000 US

D $8.50 US

17 When did T. rex disappear?

A   6,000 years ago

B   660 million years ago

C   66 million years ago

D   1066

18 What do scientists think caused T. rex to disappear?

A   An asteroid striking Earth

B   T. rex flu

C   A bigger dinosaur

D   A plague of giant dinosaur-eating locusts

19 In which movie did T. rex fight a giant gorilla?

A   *Bambi*

B   *Night at the Museum*

C   *The Sound of Music*

D   *King Kong*

20 Which of these creatures is most closely related to T. rex?

A   Frog

B   Crocodile

C   Sparrow

D   You

ANSWERS

1.	C	8.	B	15.	D
2.	C	9.	D	16.	A
3.	A	10.	C	17.	C
4.	B	11.	B	18.	A
5.	D	12.	B	19.	D
6.	A	13.	C	20.	C
7.	C	14.	C		

HOW DID YOU SCORE?

15-20 correct answers:
Congratulations! You're a real T. rexpert!

10-14 correct answers: Almost there.
Read this book again to boost your score.

5-9 correct answers: You really need to
spend a little more time with T. rex!

1-4 correct answers: Hmm. You *do*
know it's a dinosaur, don't you?

The publishers would like to thank the following sources for their kind
permission to reproduce the pictures in this book.

Key: t=Top, b=Bottom, m=Middle, l=Left and r=Right.

Page 1 Carlton Books; 2–3 background Shutterstock; 2–3 foreground
Carlton Books; 4–5 Carlton Books; 6–7 Carlton Books; 8–9 Carlton
Books; 11 Sahua d/Shutterstock; 12l Louie Psihoyos/Getty Images;
12r JoeLena/iStockphoto.com; 13t Andrew Kerr; 13b Carlton Books;
14 Andrew Kerr; 16 Jonathan Blair/Corbis; 17t Linda Bucklin/Shutterstock;
17b Charles Brutlag/Shutterstock; 18–19 Shutterstock; 19t Alex Ramsay/
Alamy; 19m Shutterstock; 20–21 Jean-Baptiste Rabouan/Hemis/Corbis;
22 Crazytang/iStockphoto.com; 23 Louie Psihoyos/Getty Images;
24 Carlton Books.

Every effort has been made to acknowledge correctly and contact the
source and/or copyright holder of each picture and Carlton Books Limited
apologises for any unintentional errors or omissions, which will be corrected
in future editions of this book.